On Purpose: How To Discover Your Purpose Using 12 Proven Tools

MOSES OMOJOLA

DEDICATION

Dedicated to anyone who is ready to step out of confusion and proceed on the journey of discovering whom God created him or her to do.

MOSES OMOJOLA

CONTENTS

ACKNOWLEDGMENTS

My profound gratitude goes to the almighty God for the uncommon wisdom given to me to unravel the mystery of destiny and life purpose, thereby adding value to lives.

Introduction

Bravo, I welcome to the life of knowing what God created you to do as you read this great book on Destiny Discovery and Mentoring. This is a special book in which I will be guiding you practically to unwrap your divine destiny or life purpose. Come to think of it, why did God orchestrate these special tools to be on your path in this crucial stage of your life? I believe God is up to something!

God's word says:

1 Cor 12:7-10

But the manifestation of the Spirit is given to every man to profit withal. For to one is given by the Spirit the word of wisdom; to another the word of knowledge by the same Spirit; To another faith by the same Spirit; to another the gifts of healing by the same Spirit; To another the working of miracles; to another prophecy; to another discerning of spirits; to another divers kinds of tongues; to another the interpretation of tongues:

Gal 5:22-23

But the fruit of the Spirit is love, joy, peace, longsuffering, gentleness, goodness, faith, Meekness, temperance: In this chapter, you are going to make decisions that will affect your life for good. Therefore you need the Holy Spirit to activate some of His gifts in you so as to enable you make the right decisions. After discovering who you are from this chapter, it is expected of you that you display Christ character which is embedded in the nine Fruits of the Spirit, as you journey through your divine assignment to fulfill your life purpose. Once again, this is Holy Spirit chapter, so I welcome you to School of the Spirit. Your destiny or life purpose has been a mystery before now. In this chapter, I will be taking you through the eleven amazing tools that will make you know who you are. God's word says:

Ephesians 2:10

That we ourselves are God's Craftsmanship, created in Christ Jesus to do good works, which God prepared in advance for us to do.

Job 10:8

Your hands shaped me and made me. To enable you know who you are, your shape, your make –up and your divine destiny, I will like us to consider five characteristics namely: Your Values, Uniqueness, Personal Vision, Personal Mission and Goals.

Test Objectives

1. To help you discover who you are, your make – up and shape for your divine assignment.

2. To help you discover your divine assignment, real work, career and best fit in life.

3. To take you out of every form of confusion and frustration surrounding your calling and jobs. 4. To help you develop a basic destiny profile for yourself. What do I mean by Destiny Profile? A Destiny Profile is a life manual, similar to equipment instruction manual, with which you can guide yourself through life and become successful, fulfilled, fruitful, and significant.

Instructions

Articulate all that you have read before getting to this very sensitive part of this book. Of course, this is one of the most important messages this book is intended to pass on to you so that your life will never remain the same again. This book is designed to be a turning point in your life. Pray strongly and ask God to open your heart, reveal every detail you need to know about yourself, and help you put the right answers down in your workbook, as you go through this exercise to discover your divine destiny, career, real work not jobs, and your best fit in life. Where you're asked to select, put them down in order of preference, that is, 1st, 2nd, 3rd, etc.

Tool 1: Identify Your Values

Your value has to do with your understanding. Answer these questions:

1. What is important to me?

2. What does God say about me?

3. What do I inherently believe? These are the things that set you apart.

Your Uniqueness

David declares in Psalm 139 by the spirit of God that you are "fearfully and wonderfully made." In the next steps, I will lead you into gaining an understanding of your uniqueness as an individual. Your uniqueness consists of the followings:

1. Your Personality

2. Your Spiritual Giftedness

3.   Your divine work passions

4.   Your Life's (Personal) Roles

Tool 2: Unwrap Your Gifts

Ask yourself this question: What am I gifted to do? Please, go through the following gifts inventory carefully and identify the best 3-4 gifts you may have been given by God: Administration/Guidance

Apostle Celibacy Craftsmanship/Artisan iscernment/DistinguishSpirits Encouragement Evangelism Exhortation Faith Giving Healing Helps/Service Hospitality Intercession/Prayer Knowledge Leadership Mercy/Compassion Miracles Missionary Music pastoring/Shepherding Prophesy Teaching Tongues(interpreting) Tongues(speaking) Wisdom Writing

Tool: 3 Monitor Your Heartbeat

3.1 Ask Yourself The Following Questions:

What motivate my heart? What do I have passion for? What do I love to do? Clarify what you really love to do. Remember: Your heart is the real you! Your heart represents the center of your motivation, desires and inclinations. To serve God's will and fulfill your destiny on earth, you must let your heartbeat motivates you for your Divine Assignment. Please, ponder on these questions: Why do I say what I say? Why do I feel the way I feel? Why do I act the way I act?

3.2 Key To Understanding Your Heartbeat:

Now look at your past accomplishments, and list your accomplishments since childhood. Let this list cover your accomplishments at home, school, work, church, etc. By accomplishment, I mean things you enjoyed doing and things you believe you did well. You must give specific details about those things you did well and forget what other people think about them. More explicitly, classify the highlights of what you did well to cover your primary school years, as teenager, in college, early twenties and thirties, up to your present age. Please, list them out comprehensively in your workbook.

3.3 Discover The Motivation Direction Of Your Heart

From the list below, select 3 activities you know you will love to be involved in: Design and develop Pioneer Organize Operate/Maintain Serve/Help Acquire and possess Excel Influence Perform Improve Repair Lead and be in charge Persevere Follow the rules Prevail.

Tool 4: Apply Your Abilities (Skills and Talents)

At this point you ask yourself: What natural talents, skills and abilities do I have? Here you want to appreciate your natural endowment including vocational skills. Researchers have proved that you have 500 to 700 abilities as a human being.

Among the abilities, talents and skills listed below, which 3 of them do you think you are actually good at?

Entertaining ability Recruiting Interview Researching Artistic Graphics Evaluating Planning Managing Analyzing Building Coaching Computing Communicating Connecting Consulting Cooking Coordinating Designing Developing Directing Editing

Encouraging Engineering Forecasting Implementing Improving Influencing

Leading Learning Mentoring Motivating Negotiating Operating Organizing Performing Pioneering Performing Repairing Counseling Teaching Promoting Resourcing Serving Strategizing Teaching Translating Traveling Visualizing Welcoming Writing Feeding Recall Mechanical operating Resourceful Counting Classifying Public Relations Composing Landscaping Decorating ability.

Plug In Your Personality

Now I want you to Plug in your personality and see how God has designed you to fix perfectly into your Divine Assignment. God expects you to do something that naturally comes to you, not by struggling or much difficulty. You need to feel comfortable while working, using the least possible effort and time, and have the work professionally done. I want you to work in the area that is suited for your personality. Now, ask yourself where does my personality best suit me to serve. Don't panic, I will work it out with you.

Tool 5: Know Your Personality Style

Ask yourself what personality style do I have? There are four types of personality style, from which God designed you to have one. No personality is bad. A man who has anger in his spirit is not good as a greeter in the church but he is great as a prayer warrior in the church, because when he uses his anger to pray against Satan, Satan will somersault ten times at each screaming.

The Four Personality Styles:

Achievements/Planned person: Make a thorough and accurate Leader.

Achievements/Spontaneous person: Make a good Leader for large projects.

Relationships/Planned person: Makes a good team Leader. Relationships/Spontaneous person: Makes a good promoter and recruiter.

A person who has achievement/Planned personality style will be characterized by focusing on results and will operate best with goals in view.

A person who has Achievements/Spontaneous personality will like to get jobs done and will prefer wide variety of responsibilities.

A relationships/planned person will be fond of enjoying familiar relationship but will prefer to interact with people in defined setting.

While someone with Relationships/Spontaneous personality style will be characterized by being very conversational and will enjoy moving between varieties of activities.

My Personality Style

What personality style do I have? My personality style is Achievements/Planned. This implies that I am a thorough and accurate Leader. Of course, there is no gainsaying that I am a proven administrator. I once worked as administrator in an establishment where my immediate and only boss's personality style was Relationships/Spontaneous. He was a good promoter and had excellent skills in building relationships.

Tool 6: Know Your Temperament

Now what character do you display as you live your life daily? Let us examine the five characters below. I will explain them and you will then rate yourself on these temperament scales. How do you see yourself?

Are You An Extroverted Or Introverted Person?

Extroverted – Get drained when alone, Recharged by being with people, and achieves more when with people.

Introverted –Being alone recharges him, being with people drains him, and achieves more when alone. Prefers quiet environment.

Are You A Thinker Or Feeler?

Thinker - Makes decisions based on facts. Feeler – Makes decision based on feeling or intuition.

Are You A Routine Or Variety Person?

Routine – Likes following a set pattern or procedure all the time. Variety – Prefers diversity or changes in doing things, and get bored repeating the same thing.

Are You A Self- Controlled Or Self-Expressive Person?

Self – controlled: Always control his reaction, keeps matter within him, tolerate things or situations. Self – expressive: Like to express himself openly, and expresses how he feels concerning issues.

Are You A Co-Operative Or Competitive Person?

Co-operative: Like to cooperate, support a system, and hate competition. Competitive: Born competitor; believe in himself, and like to compete with an existing fit. He feels he can do things like somebody else or do better.

My Temperament I am more of Introverted, Thinker, and Self – expressive. I love Variety and Competition.

Tool 7: Articulate Your Unique Personality Traits

From the list below, which of these help you respond to other people and to opportunities? I am:

Bold Talkative Compassionate Precautionary Venturesome Decisive Empathetic Hospitable Steadfast Eager.Accommodating Careful Self-assured Enthusiastic Loyal Easygoing Orderly Organized Persuasive Responsive Open Minded Mild Sincere Restless Big picture Oriented Gentle Quiet Results focused Flexible Humble Earnest Fast paced Freewheeling Meek Reserved Intense Visionary Yielding Shy Meticulous.

My Personality Traits

Talkative, Compassionate, Organized, Results focused, & Visionary.

Tool 8: Examine Your Experiences

Now I want you to examine your experiences. Examining your experiences will help you review your history to discover how God has prepared you for a unique assignment that only you can do. Ask yourself the following questions and honestly supply the answers:

1. What are the Spiritual experiences I have had? These are meaningful decisions you have taken in the past and the time you've had with God.

2. What are the Painful experiences I have had? These are problems, hurts, trials that you have encountered in life that you have learnt something from. Be informed that God never waste a hurt, He allowed it under His permissive will so that you can use it to minister to people going through the same hurt in life.

3. What are the Educational experiences I have had? These should include a recall of your

favourite subjects in school and your educational trend.

4. What are the Ministry experiences I have had? This is an account of how you have served God and the positions you've held in the past.

5. What are the Working experiences I have had? Here you recall experiences you've had in doing secular work or your craftsmanship in the past.

6. In what areas have I serve humanity in the past? Take account of those areas you've been moved by your heart of compassion to show kindness to people or do charity in the past.

Tool 9: Determine Your Destiny Function And Forms

Every person existing on planet earth today has a destiny function and several forms of destiny. There is a being part and a doing part of your destiny.

Destiny Function:

This is the being part of your destiny. It is the predetermined and permanent part of your destiny.

Forms Of Destiny: This is the doing part of your destiny. It is the flexible and changing part of your destiny.

Ego Drive And Soul Drive: Are you driven by your ego (Opinion of yourself/Worldly desire, fleshly desire) or your soul (spirit or heart)?

Now, consider this: A certain Lecturer: 1. Lectures in a University 2. Writes a book 3. Speaks in conference about the book, and

4. Holds Radio & TV programmes talking to audience about his book.

In all these roles he acts as a teacher. So Teaching is the function of his destiny. He serves people and makes money from lecturing, writing books, motivational speaking, and talking to greater audience on radio and television. These various activities he involves in: Lecturing, writing books, Motivational speaking, and talking to Radio and Television audience are his Forms of destiny. Now, list out your function and forms of destiny to the glory of God.

Tool 10: Identify And Unlock Your Destiny From Persons

Here, I don't want you to miss the people that God gave to you to help you identify and walk in your destiny. God gave you this people to help you achieve your destiny. Now, Who are the people that you worked with in the past and what values or pains, and lessons have you learnt from them? List out your answers in your workbook.

From Situations I want you to agree with me that your destiny has been locked to certain situations in your journey through life. I mean in your effort to succeed and walk in your destiny, you have gone through some unpleasant situations, which I wouldn't want you to complain about or give up. I want you to persist in it, do rightly, and walk through whatever difficulties you may face until you reach your destiny. Now, in your workbook, list out all the unpleasant situations or experiences you've had in your past.

Tool 11: Cast Your Vision and Life Mission

Finally, let me put you through how you can cast your own vision. Your vision will make you stand out among billions of people. When you know your divine assignment; your destiny and the sequence of events that will make you fulfill your earthly assignment, then you will know the people God send you to, and how to reach them. At this point you can cast your personal vision. After you sincerely cast your life vision, you will never again be confused or hungry in life. Whenever people threaten to walk out of your life, you ask them to walk. If people want to put you on the wrong track, you talk to yourself, Moses; this is what God designed you to do before the foundation of the world. This man was not there when God gave you the assignment, so look out. What follows next is a smile on your face. May be you continue to wonder why great and workaholic men like Bishop David Oyedepo of Living Faith Church, Nigeria, are always seen beaming with smile. It is because of the beauty of their vision. Even as I'm on my computer now, using the keyboard to type this things down for you as I'm receiving this inspiration, I'm beaming with smile, because I'm working in my own garden of Eden, my passion, my best fit in life, a form of my destiny, and anointing of ease is increasing daily upon me to dress it well and keep it.

Come to think of it, the normal way of writing a book is to write everything on a piece of paper first, before typing it into the computer. But this is another situation whereby you just boot up your computer, go to Microsoft word environment and begin to type in directly the inspiration you are receiving from God. Which is better? Beloved, knowing your divine assignment will do more than this for you. Oh! What a suit thing to know where you belong and key into it. When you locate your niche, fatigue will seize to be an English word. I want to see you in this great realm after completing this great book. I define Vision as the ability to see your future from God's perspective; it is God's preferable future.

Personal Vision focuses on the future; it is God designed and man discovered. It flows from the redemptive heart of God and it reflects God's unique, specific call to an individual. Some struggle with the concept of Vision, but throughout history God has birthed vision into the hearts and lives of His people. In generation past, men and women have heard from God, and by faith, have stepped out and trusted God. From Nehemiah to Apostle Paul, from Luther to John Knox, down to today; personal vision has been documented in biblical and contemporary history.

Vision involves passion! It motivates and captures the individual. It is what the heart yearns to see accomplished. Vision leads to leadership in the garden God made you to keep and dress. Bishop David Oyedepo says of vision, "Leadership has to do with a sincere mission to the well being of others" He stressed further that every true vision must be centered on God. Maybe you have been suffering for a long time, hear what Pastor Matthew Ashimolowo says, "Vision is the answer to defeating poverty" A man with vision and strong passions will never be hungry before he moves into a life of affluence.

Instruction

To understand your Personal Vision and mission, relax yourself now, and take a deep breath. Now, with a deep thought, answers the following question to the best of your ability in your workbook.

1. What are my values? What do I attach importance to or what is important to me in life?

2. What does God says about me?

3. What do I essentially believe?

4. What are the things that excite or motivate or interest me (passions)?

5. What spiritual gifts do I believe that I have?

6. What personality do I have? (Qualities I possess or things that set me apart)

7. What personal roles have I played or positions have I held in the past in life?

8. Who are the people and circumstances that have most shaped my life and ministry?

9. What are the character qualities I most admire, and desire for God to shape into my life?

10. People who know me well, believe I am most used by God when I am involved in?

11. From the perspective of my ministry life, the activities I do, that I feel I am making my greatest contribution to God's Kingdom or humanity are?

12. Though I may have dismissed the thought many times before, for various reasons, at times I have felt what I really should be doing is?

13. If I knew you would not fail, what would I do for the Glory of God?

Tool 12: Time

Without mincing words, to effectively discover your life purpose, it good to consider how you've been spending your time since birth. Ask yourself these questions: What takes my time? What do I love to spend time doing? What do I do faster, easier and better than others? What do I get frustrated doing?

Evaluating your answers to these questions will further suggest where the pendulum of your life is expected to swing!

How To Get Your Unique Personalized Destiny/Business Profile

At this juncture, carefully go through all the information you have put down about yourself, make analysis and summarize them. Now, develop what I will call your Basic Destiny Profile. Then compare yours to my own Comprehensive Professionally Analyzed Personalized Destiny Profile below: Mine is a sample of the Comprehensive Professionally Analyzed Destiny Profile issued by our organization.

My Own Comprehensive Professionally Analyzed Per/sonalized Destiny Profile

Be it known that Moses Omojola DP/PH/09/0612 Divine Destiny has been duly Discovered using our Quality Assessment, Written Tests and Interview by our Destiny Mentor, and Has been awarded Professionally Analyzed Destiny Profile (Life Manual/Divine Assignment Guide) Details below

CORE VALUES: *Seeing those passing through hurts healed.* UNIQUENESS: *Gifting: Compassion, Prophecy & Administration.* **Passions**: *Helping, serving and rescuing the oppressed or the demoralized.*

Abilities: *Engineering, Encouragement, Teaching, Repairing, Writing & Documenting. Personality: Planned, Result- focused, Creative thinker.*

Life roles: *Teacher, Adm/*inistrator, Healing minister. To have satisfaction, fulfillment, significance, fruitfulness & success in life the followings are recommended:* **VISION**: *To bring those experiencing hurt in life to God for healing, teach people to live the Christian life and reach the needy world.*

MISSION: *To provide the tools to reach the lost, the sick, the oppressed and develop people into fruit bearing disciples.*

DESTINY FUNCTION: *Changing lives*

BEST FIT IN LIFE/DESTINY FORMS/DIVINE WORK/CAREER TO BE SOUGHT FOR: *Life seminar presentation/Motivational speaking, Counseling, holding Sin Intervention,*

Charity and Advocacy, Healing.

Our organization is saddled with the responsibility of helping individuals or group of people to discover their divine destiny and the business God uniquely create them to do, strategize and start to success.

Take A Step Now

After we help you to discover your destiny and unique business, you'll no longer be confused about life. We bring out the hidden virtues in you and you're sought for those great roles rather you looking for employment elsewhere, with so much frustrations attached tojob employment. Be aware that your divine assignment - destiny forms, best-fit in life, divine work is different from your career, profession or those things that have wrongfully occupy you in life and worn you out. Your divine assignment refreshes you, makes you happier daily, significance and put food on your table while you become more passionate daily.

You can't discover your destiny and not be a writer, an author of many books and a speaker. You'll have something unique to contribute to humanity and have a unique message or subject that must announce you to your generation. This book is very rich. However to complement the wisdom you've acquired from this book, I'll suggest you contact me to go with you a step further. I will put you through, mentor and coach you to success.

Visit my website for more information.

How To Start Your Divine Assignment

Now that you have discovered your divine destiny, it is mandatory that you have knowledge of how you should begin your life mission or ministry. The path to fulfilling your purpose must be in conformity with how our Lord Jesus enters into His earthly ministry.

How Jesus Began His Work

Before praying about your life mission you must understand how Jesus started His earthly ministry, carried out his divine assignment and fulfill his destiny on earth. At the age of thirty, Jesus knew He had an instinct to begin the journey of fulfilling His destiny. He needed to follow some divine order. So He had to go all the way to River Jordan to meet John the Baptist for baptism. This was somebody Jesus knew was lower in hierarchy to Him. Jesus did this because He knew that humility comes before promotion. Jesus got baptized, received the Holy Spirit, and God announced Him as His beloved son in whom He is ever well pleased.

Matt 3:16-17

When He had been baptized, Jesus came up immediately from the water; and behold, the heavens were opened to Him, and He saw the Spirit of God descending like a dove and alighting upon Him. And suddenly a voice came from heaven, saying, "This is My beloved Son, in whom I am well pleased. Jesus' baptism was followed by His time of trial in the wilderness, with devil trying to truncate His destiny.

Matt 4:1-2

Then Jesus was led up by the Spirit into the wilderness to be tempted by the devil. And when He had fasted forty days and forty nights, afterward He was hungry. Thank God that His spirit was with Him. At the end of forty days, Satan became exhausted, so he departed from Jesus. At this stage, the Bible says that angels came and ministered unto Him. What did the Holy angels minister unto Him? They came to congratulate Jesus Christ for having overcome the devil, also to put Him on the part of fulfilling His divine assignment. Heaven agreed to back Him up, and gave Him signs and wonders ministry.

Matt 4:9-11

Then Jesus said to him, "Away with you, Satan! For it is written, 'You shall worship the LORD your God, and Him only you shall serve.' " Then the devil left Him, and behold, angels came and ministered to Him. Jesus then began His preaching career, starting from the known to the unknown. He started with the message God gave to John the Baptist: "Repent, for the kingdom of heaven is at hand".

Matt 4:17

From that time Jesus began to preach and to say, "Repent, for the kingdom of heaven is at hand. Jesus knew that He needed some subordinates to run His earthly vision with. As a leader He needed to build a team to have a successful ministry, so the spirit of God helped Him to recruit four disciples quickly. Peter the rock was the first to be recruited.

Matt 4:18-20 *And Jesus, walking by the Sea of Galilee, saw two brothers; Simon called Peter, and Andrew his brother, casting a net into the sea; for they were fishermen. 19 Then He said to them, "Follow Me, and I will make you fishers of men." 20 They immediately left their nets and followed Him.* As soon as Jesus got a team, He began to preach and teach and heal all manners of sicknesses and diseases.

Matt 4:23-25 *And Jesus went about all Galilee, teaching in their synagogues, preaching the gospel of the kingdom, and healing all kinds of sickness and all kinds of disease among the people. Then His fame went throughout all Syria; and they brought to Him all sick people who were afflicted with various diseases and torments, and those who were demon-possessed, epileptics, and paralytics; and He healed them. Great multitudes followed Him from Galilee, and from Decapolis, Jerusalem, Judea, and beyond the Jordan.*

The Golden Ladder

Our Patriarch – Jacob saw in a vision, a ladder that linked earth and heaven, through which angels were ascending and descending. And when he had that encounter with God, his life was transformed forever:

Gen 28:10-12 *Now Jacob went out from Beersheba and went toward Haran. So he came to a certain place and stayed there all night, because the sun had set. And he took one of the stones of that place and put it at his head, and he lay down in that place to sleep. Then he dreamed, and behold, a ladder was set up on the earth, and its top reached to heaven; and there the angels of God were ascending and descending on it.* Let me state clearly to you again that your divine destiny is in Christ, and you are here on earth to fulfill your own part of God's purpose. So it is pertinent that you become a believer, that is, someone who accepts the Lord Jesus Christ as his Lord and saviour, and is committed to living a spirit - filled life. Below are the seven steps in the golden ladder you must climb as you journey along your path of destiny:

Step 1: Baptism

Confess the Lord Jesus Christ as your Lord and saviour, get baptized in the right way by immersion, and seek Holy Ghost baptism.

Step 2: Life In The Wilderness

After your water and Holy Ghost baptism, as a believer, the spirit of God will lead you into the wilderness as He did to Jesus Christ. This is your period of sanctification by the Holy Spirit; discipleship – a time in which you are learning to become a Christian. Maybe your body is forty years old when you are led to Christ. Your Soul is about thirty years old, while your spirit man is just five years old. Your times in the wilderness is a time to feed your spirit man with spiritual food – the Word of God - so that it can attain your real age – forty years. Life in the wilderness is your time of travail like a pregnant woman who is about to deliver her child. It is the time that you wrestle with the devil. God's word says "the kingdom of God suffereth violence, and the violent taketh it by force". This is a period that the devil will want to convince you that it is better for you to backslide and follow him rather than follow your creator. This period will come in form of various kinds of temptations, trials and afflictions orchestrated by Satan to make you miss heaven. The Devil is a liar. So you must stand your ground like Jesus did. By total commitment and total worship you will overcome by the blood of the lamb.

Step 3: Devil's Departure

After the Devil has tempted you in so many ways and you are more than conqueror, he will depart from you. Satanic influence will cease for a moment in your life. The spirit of confusion that has been troubling your life will varnish and your eyes of understanding will be enlightened. Now, you will be sensitive to spiritual things and know the hope of your calling in Christ Jesus. Like the children of Issachar, you will understand the times ahead of you and know what God want you to do.

MOSES OMOJOLA

52

Step 4: Angelic Visitation

As soon as Devil depart from you during your sanctification period, God will send angels to you to help you accomplish your life mission. Hear what God's word says:

Ex 23:20-21

Behold, I send an Angel before you to keep you in the way and to bring you into the place which I have prepared. Beware of Him and obey His voice The angels will give you the key to understanding every mystery about your life purpose; provided you subject yourself day and night to the leading of the Holy Spirit.

Step 5: The Beginning Of Acting

As a child of God, the book of Acts of the Apostles continues with you. After your fellowship with the ministering spirits, God will give you extraordinary power to begin your work using your tool of ministry. This is the kind of anointing Peter spoke of when he was preaching to Cornelius family in the book of Acts:

Acts 10:38

And God anointed Jesus of Nazareth with the Holy Spirit and with power, who went about doing good and healing all who were oppressed by the devil, for God was with Him. If your tool of ministry is your mouth, you may be a preacher, a teacher or an entertainer, etc. Maybe your tool of ministry is your hand; you are good in craftsmanship like Bezalel and Aholiab (Exodus 31). Whatever your tool of ministry is, God has chosen you to be "first among many brethren", that is, a leader in your generation. This is the stage where you begin from the known to the unknown. Jesus started with the same message that was preached by John the Baptist. Many Pastors started their preaching or teaching careers with the sermons of their mentors. As you continue to act within your calling, I see your fame increase abroad, in Jesus' name.

Step 6: Gathering Your Twelve

Whatever your ministry or calling, God wants you to work with a team that the Holy Spirit will help you to select. God wants you to have men like Peter, James and John as members of your inner caucus. Peter had strong ability to deputize, James, arguably the most matured disciple, had unequal skills in resolving crisis among the Christendom, and John showed the greatest love and loyalty to Jesus by being fond of Him; which helped him to write the book of Revelation. To God, Jesus was His beloved son, but to Jesus, John was His own beloved son in whom He was well pleased, so He revealed to him the things that were yet to come. Prayerfully choose your team of twelve. This is very important if you want to have spiritual success, and not canal success.

Step 7: Taking Territories

A leader is not expected to walk alone. When you have gotten your team, you are now the balanced leader that God designed you to be. A king has an entourage. A president also have followers, so that when the king or the president is visiting any place, some of the entourage go before him, some go behind him while some walk at pal with him. They all play different roles, which together help the king or the president to be adored with honour. Together with your team, you will visualize, organize, plan, coordinate and direct people to accomplish the task God deposits in you heart to do. This is the actual beginning of your ministry and a gallant step to taking territories, and living a life of significance.

Getting Your Unique Message And Products

Every man must have a clear message God designed him to communicate to his generation. It is your message that will make you unique among millions of competitors. If you ask me what my message is, I will tell you my message is compassion. Most pastors pity the needy and do compassion by helping them, but they don't teach it as their subject. I teach exclusively compassion and the seven results of compassion. Let me remind you of some great men and their unique subjects: Billy Graham – Evangelism, Mensah Otabil – Leadership, David Oyedepo – Wisdom, Benny Hinn – Healing, Kenneth Hagin – Faith, Kenneth Copland – Prosperity.

Some men of God and some church members copied the voice, style of ministering and even the hairdo of their mentors, thereby hiding whom they are and limiting their destiny. People would prefer buying their mentor's tape for life rather than such copycat own, because of absence of uniqueness. You must seek the face of God to know vividly what your message is, and whom you are sent to serve and affect in your generation.

<u>Other Books By Moses Omojola Available in Paperback and Ebook format on Amazon:</u>

- How To Break Into Your Calling

- Understanding The Mystery of Destiny

- Surprise Healing: How to activate the miracles in your spirit

- Living Beyond Yourself: How to navigate into success and significance

- Flight To Purpose: A Step By Step Guide To Your Assignment

- Repositioning The Church: Morals And Teachings

- How To Pray In The Holy Ghost And Win All Battles

- Destiny Pilot 1: Introduction and Destiny

Recovery

- Destiny Pilot 2: The Mistakes

- Destiny Pilot 3: The Advice

- How To Harmonize Your Destiny With Divine Intervention

- How To Cope With Thorns In The Flesh: Turning Barriers To Success
- Prayer To Discover Your Purpose and How To Start Life Assignment

- Leadership and Sin Intervention: How Not To Treat Offenders

- How To Discover Your Divine Destiny and Total Breakthroughs

- faith

- 21 Keys to Miracles in Helpless Situations: How to pray when you can't pray
- How To Make Heaven: Eliminating caricature, making the path straight

- How To Break The Yoke Of Life: Finding your way to freedom, health, wealth and fulfillment
- There Is Church Everywhere But Love Is Not Everywhere – Says Holy Spirit

To find any of these books online, visit author's website or search on Amazon or Google, for the book title. E.g search: How To Break Into Your Calling by Moses Omojola.

Thank you.

MOSES OMOJOLA

Author of 'How To Discover Your Divine Destiny and Total Breakthroughs' and many other great books.

E-Mail: support@jomakinspublishing.com

Website: www.jomakinspublishing.com

BOOK TAGS

meaning of life, goal setting, purpose of life, on purpose, purpose, self improvement, self confidence, career change, career counseling, dream meaning, my destiny, my future, destiny, leadership skills, looking for a job, careers, career counseling, healing scriptures, scriptures on healing, goal setting, purpose of life, self improvement, destiny, leadership skills, looking for a job, careers, divine intervention, sermons, health and wellness, getting pregnant, vision, the vision, what does my dream mean, depression treatment, my destiny, dream meaning, purpose of life, careers, dreams, vision, how to choose a career, choosing career, vision statement, my destiny, job search, dream meaning, what is the purpose of life, on purpose, purpose of life, destiny, vision statement, career change, career counseling, career coaching, healing prayer, prayers for strength, how to choose a career, choosing career, career finder, vision statement, my destiny, job search, dream meaning, what is the purpose of life, mission and vision, what does my dream mean, leadership training, how to choose a career, choosing career, career finder, vision statement, my destiny, job search, dream meaning, what is the purpose of life, mission and vision, what does my dream mean, career coach, ordained, christian counseling, human rights, leadership training, social justice issues, divine intervention, church of christ, spiritual gifts test, ordained, evangelist, youth group, family christian store, morning devotions, christian counseling, career coach, power of prayer, bible study, bible studies, find a job, job opportunities, job seekers, leadership development, sermons, sermon, success stories, success story, the holy spirit, business opportunity, business opportunities, rehab, social anxiety, retirement planning, pastor, christian dating, evening prayer, morning prayer, health and wellness, health and fitness, christian, dream interpretation, dream interpretation, symptoms of depression, symptoms of anxiety, signs of depression, what is the purpose of life, what is the meaning of life, symptoms of stress, stress symptoms, how to relieve stress, how to reduce stress, how to manage stress, how to cope with stress

For Comments, Coaching and Consulting:

To help you:

- Discover your destiny or life purpose, Cast life Vision and Goals.

- Discover 3-4 profitable businesses you are created to do to have wealth, live healthy and have inner peace.

- Develop your Comprehensive Professionally Analyzed Destiny/Business Profile issued by our organization.

- Teach you how to write book, write great, voluminous and over 20 books.

  - Self-publish your book for you.

  -Convert your book to Ebook and Paperback format, upload and sell on Amazon, Barnes & Noble, Apple store, Kobo, etc.

  -Edit and Proofread books.

  -Design Website and Blog.

- Consulting on life issues, business and health matters, book writing, publishing.

CONTACT:

MOSES OMOJOLA

Author of '**How To Discover Your Divine Destiny and Total Breakthroughs**' and many other great books.

E-Mail: support@jomakinspublishing.com

Website: www.jomakinspublishing.com

About the Author

Moses Omojola is the author of the bestselling book: "How to discover your divine destiny and total breakthroughs". He spent 16 years working as an Engineer in the Oil and Gas industry before he was divinely conscripted into his divine assignment. He is also an international speaker, counselor, destiny mentor, business and wellness coach. His specialties are hidden truths, divine assignment, justice, success and leadership.

He runs workshops to help people discover their destiny, the unique business God created them to do, how to start and succeed. He also counsel individuals empathetically on issues relating to destiny, business, employment, health, relationships, and many more, using the awesome power inherent in their destiny, and assist many to become writers and self – publish many books.

www.ingramcontent.com/pod-product-compliance
Lightning Source LLC
Chambersburg PA
CBHW061200180526
45170CB00002B/884